WESTMINSTER SCHOOLS

SMYTHE GAMBRELL
LIBRARY

PRESENTED BY

Glynnis Roberts

SCIENCE FUN WITH A HOMEMADE CHEMISTRY SET

Rose Wyler
Pictures by Pat Stewart

JULIAN MESSNER
A Division of Simon & Schuster, Inc., New York

Text copyright © 1987 by Rose Wyler
Illustrations copyright © 1987 by Pat Stewart

JULIAN MESSNER and colophon are trademarks of Simon & Schuster, Inc.

10 9 8 7 6 5 4 3 2 1 Lib. ed.
10 9 8 7 6 5 4 3 2 1 Pbk. ed.

Manufactured in the United States of America
Design by Lisa Hollander

Library of Congress Cataloguing in Publication Data
Wyler, Rose.
Science fun with a homemade chemistry set.

Summary: Introduces some basic concepts of chemistry
through simple experiments with such household supplies
as baking powder, soap, and vinegar.
1. Chemistry—Experiments—Juvenile literature.
(1. Chemistry—Experiments.   2. Experiments)   I. Title.
QD38.W95 1987   542   86-21868
ISBN 0-671-55575-8 Lib. ed.
ISBN 0-671-55570-7 Pbk. ed.

FOREWORD

Science provides a way of looking at the world around you to find out how it works. All the things around you are made of chemicals. This is true of things that you can taste, touch, smell, and see and things you can't see, like air. Scientists mix different chemicals together and change them completely. Sometimes they make something entirely new, like plastic.

You too can work with chemicals and make things from them, the way a scientist does. In this book there are real experiments you can do with materials from around the house. The experiments are easy to do and so much fun, you will want to try them all.

Lewis Love
Great Neck Public Schools
Long Island, New York

ACKNOWLEDGMENTS

The author and publisher wish to thank the people who read the manuscript of this book and made suggestions: Lewis Love, Great Neck, New York, Public Schools; Joseph Alper; and the many young "helpers" who tried the experiments.

Other Books by Rose Wyler

The Giant Golden Book of Astronomy
Prove It!
Secrets in Stones [all written with Gerald Ames]
Science Fun with Mud and Dirt
Science Fun with Peanuts and Popcorn
Science Fun with Toy Boats and Planes

CONTENTS

Better Than Magic

Remember how Cinderella's fairy godmother waved her magic wand? Cinderella's rags turned into silk. A pumpkin became a splendid coach.

Chemists do better than that. From air, water, and coal, they make silky cloth. From stone and clay, they make metals for cars and planes.

Instead of waving magic wands, chemists take substances apart, then use the parts to make new materials. They bring about changes called *chemical reactions*.

You will gain this power, too, if you learn to experiment with chemicals. Working at home or in school, you can bring about many exciting chemical reactions. You can make plastics, liquids that change color, crystals, giant bubbles, lively gases. Ready to start?

Making a Chemistry Set

The kitchen can be your lab. But anyplace with a table will do, for you'll be working with jars, cups, spoons, pots, and pans.

For chemicals you'll use cooking and cleaning supplies. You can store them in baby food jars. But check with a grown-up before you use any household supplies. When you experiment with them, don't put them in your mouth. And remember to wash your hands when you have finished.

You can keep all your equipment in large boxes or shopping bags. You'll build up a fine chemistry set in this way.

Plastics—Chemicals That Can Be Shaped

Many bags, boxes, jars, and dishes that you use in experiments are made of polymers. You probably call them plastics. You wear plastics, too. Sneakers are made of them; so are some raincoats, boots, and shoes. In making flat things, melted plastic is pressed into sheets. Other things are made by pouring plastics into molds or over forms.

Ask your mother if you can use some nail polish. It contains a chemical that's like a plastic. Make a little rain hat from it and you'll see how a plastic can be shaped.

Take some modeling clay and shape a doll's hat from it. Paint the clay with nail polish. Let it dry. Then paint it again. Do this three times. After the polish is hard, peel it off the clay. And there's the hat!

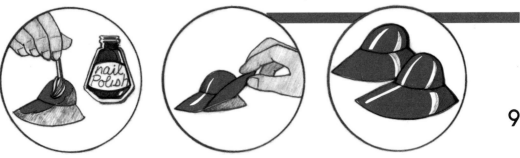

From Goo to Glue

Most plastics are made in factories with special chemicals and big, heavy equipment. But here's one kind you can make. It's casein plastic. You'll need to use a stove. So be sure a grown-up is around while you work.

Slowly heat 1 cup of skimmed milk with 2 tablespoons of white vinegar. Keep stirring until the mixture thickens and lumps form. Then take it off the stove.

Keep stirring as long as lumps are forming. The lumps, called curds, are casein. Strain them out and throw away the liquid. Now you can use the curds to make a plastic.

The plastic you make from casein is liquid. It's so sticky you can make glue from it.

Put the curds in a jar. Add 2 tablespoons of water and ½ teaspoon of baking soda. The mixture bubbles and changes into gooey white glue.

Paste two sheets of paper together to test the glue. When it's dry, try pulling the papers apart. The papers stick, don't they? The glue is very strong. It's like the white glue sold in stores. The chemical you have made really works!

What Are Chemicals Made of?

Every chemical is made of tiny invisible particles called *atoms*. But atoms are not all alike. There are over a hundred different kinds.

Some things are made of only one kind of atom. They are called *elements*. Copper is an element. So is oxygen, a gas in the air. Most chemicals are made of two or more different elements that are joined together. These chemicals are called *compounds*.

When chemicals change, atoms are shifted around. This happens when you make casein glue. You take different atoms from casein and from baking soda and join them together to make a new compound.

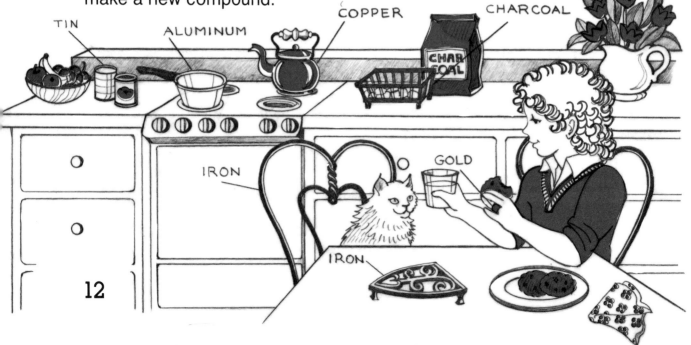

12

Do you have any old, dull pennies? The dull film on them forms as oxygen atoms from the air join copper atoms in the pennies. But you can separate the oxygen from the copper.

Put some dull pennies in a dish. Sprinkle salt on them. Add a few drops of vinegar. The dull film breaks down as oxygen atoms in it join atoms in the salt and vinegar mixture. Suddenly the pennies shine like new.

Red Liquid Trick

Some chemicals come apart easily. That happens to bleaching powder, the kind used in washing clothes. Wet the powder, and oxygen atoms in it are set free. They are lively atoms. They'll take the dirt and sometimes the color out of cloth.

The powder breaks down so fast you can use it in a trick. It will change the color of a red liquid.

Before doing the trick, ask a grown-up to put about a tablespoon of bleaching powder in a glass. Spread it so it doesn't show. Fill another glass with water and add a few drops of red food coloring to it.

Tell your friends you will change the color of the liquid. Then pour the red liquid over the bleach in the other glass. Presto! The red color vanishes.

Magic? No, something better—a chemical reaction.

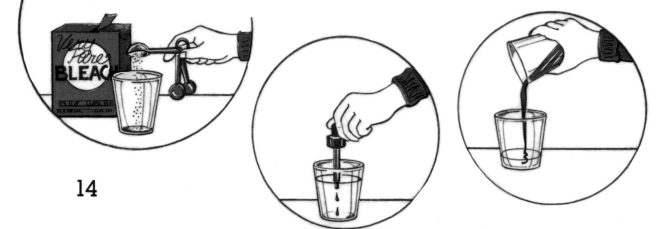

Now You See It;
Now You Don't

There it is, right before your eyes—a spoonful of sugar. Stir it into a glass of water and it vanishes. Not a speck can be seen, even with a magnifying glass. The sugar has *dissolved*. It has broken into invisible particles. These particles are called *molecules*. They are the smallest particles that are still sugar. When the sugar dissolves, the sugar molecules spread through the water.

Sugar molecules are made of still smaller particles—atoms. All chemicals are like that. They are made of molecules that are made of atoms.

The sugar molecule is made of three kinds of atoms—carbon, hydrogen, oxygen. These different atoms stick together even when sugar dissolves. They stay joined, so no new chemicals form. The sugar molecules just spread through the water. Let the water dry up and there's the sugar again.

Put 10 drops of sugar water on a clean pie plate. Set the plate under a light. The water soon dries up. In place of the drops there are spots —10 white spots of sugar.

16

The Holes in Water

How much sugar can you get into a glass of water that's full right to the rim? The amount will surprise you. Water molecules are not tightly packed. So there are holes in the liquid—invisible holes—and sugar molecules can get into them.

Fill a glass with cold water up to the rim. Have a broom straw on hand, or something thin, to stir with. Measure 1 teaspoon of sugar. Now slowly pour the sugar into the water as you gently stir it with the straw.

After the sugar dissolves, add a second teaspoonful. How many more can you add before the water overflows?

Do the experiment again, but this time use very warm water. Does warm water hold more sugar than cold water?

Crystal Wonders

Water molecules are always moving. Heat speeds them up, so spaces between them get bigger. That's why warm water holds more sugar than cold water.

The hotter the water is, the more sugar it will hold. Ask a grown-up to boil a cup of water and take it off the stove. Now you can dissolve nearly two cups of sugar in it.

Cool the sugar solution and the water slowly dries up. Sugar molecules are left behind. They come together and form crystals shaped like cubes. Give the crystals time and they'll grow.

Pour the cool sugar solution into three jars. Tie a paper clip to one end of a piece of string. Tie the other end around a pencil. Place a pencil across each jar with a clip and string in the water. In a few hours, small crystals will form on the string. Don't disturb them and they'll grow.

Sugar Gem Jewelry

In a month, the crystals will be as big as beans. You may want to use them as gems.

Lift a string of crystals and let it dry. Tie a long piece of string to the ends and you have a necklace of gems. Use two sets of crystals and short strings to make earrings.

How to Grow Crystals

You can also grow salt crystals.

Stir 5 teaspoons of salt into 5 tablespoons of cold water. Let the liquid stand until it clears. Then pour it into a saucer. Crystals will soon form.

After a few days, take out the biggest crystal with tweezers. Put it in a new salt solution and it will keep on growing. Repeat this again and again and you'll have a giant crystal.

To get crystals of different shapes, use other household chemicals. Ask a grown-up to help you. Try washing soda, borax, boric acid, and epsom salts. Each dissolves in boiling water. To make colored crystals, add food coloring to the water before you start. After a week or so, set all the crystals in a dish and you'll have a garden of gems.

Looks May Fool You

Suppose a mistake has been made. The sugar bowl was filled with salt and the salt shaker with sugar.

At supper that night, everyone "salts" the meat with sugar. Grown-ups "sugar" their coffee with salt. When people start to eat, what a nasty surprise they have! And dessert is worse. There's a big layer cake with thick white icing—icing that's mostly salt. Ugh!

If salt and sugar are in jars without labels, how can you tell them apart? They look alike. Both are made of white crystals that are shaped like cubes. They taste different, but you don't taste unknown chemicals. They might be harmful.

How, then, can you tell sugar from salt?

Tests for Look-alikes

In some ways sugar molecules act differently from salt molecules. The trick is to find those ways. Does one dissolve faster? Do both solutions freeze? Will sugar or salt melt? Test them and see.

A Dissolving Test. Take two small glasses the same size. Pour ¼ cup of water into each glass. Add 1 tablespoon of salt to one and 1 tablespoon of sugar to the other. Since these solutions look alike, add a different food coloring to each one. After an hour, which has more crystals in it?

A Freezing Test. Stir the solutions until they are clear. Using an ice cube tray with separate cups, pour each solution into four cups. Set the tray in the freezer for two hours. Then see if there's ice in any of the cups.

A Melting Test. (Do this with a grown-up.) Use a small frying pan. Put ¼ teaspoon of sugar on one side and ¼ teaspoon of salt on the other side. Flatten the piles. Heat the pan slowly for 3 minutes. Then take it from the stove and see what has happened to the salt and sugar.

Are these the results you get?

	Sugar	Salt
Dissolving Test (After 1 hour)	Nearly all dissolves	Nearly all dissolves
Freezing Test (After 2 hours)	Solution has frozen	Solution still liquid
Melting Test (After 3 minutes)	Melts and gets brown	Doesn't melt

Tests of this sort are used by scientists, too. They also use many other kinds of tests to identify chemicals.

Finding Hidden Chemicals

How black is black? Some black inks look as if they are pure black, yet dyes of many colors may be hidden in them. If the dyes dissolve in water, it's easy to separate them.

Have these things ready: a glass with about ½ inch of water in it, a paper towel, and a felt-tip pen with black ink. Cut a long strip from the paper towel. Put an ink mark about 2 inches from the bottom. Then place the strip on the rim of the glass with one end in the water. As water wets the strip, different dye colors appear on it above the ink mark.

Molecules of the different dyes go up the wet paper at different speeds. This separates the dyes.

Test other inks that dissolve in water in the same way. Test fruit and vegetable juices, too. How many can you find with chemicals of different colors hidden in them?

Scientists often do this type of testing. They call it *chromatography* (kro ma TOG ra fee). Now that you're handling chemicals, you may want to call it that, too—chromatography.

Telltale Colors

You have heard of acids, haven't you? They are the chemicals that give lemon juice and vinegar a sour taste. Many acids quickly change other chemicals. So scientists often use them in experiments.

An acid can change the kind of chemical that's called a *base*. Baking soda and ammonia are bases. Soap and other cleaning supplies are made with bases.

Most acids and bases dissolve in water. They form solutions that often look alike. Yet it's important to tell one kind from another.

To do this, scientists use a chemical that changes color. This type of chemical is found in many plants. One of them gives red cabbage its color.

Take two leaves of red cabbage and tear them into shreds. Have a grown-up boil a cup of water in an enamel pot. Put the cabbage in the hot water and crush the shreds with a wooden spoon. After an hour, the liquid will be purple. Pour it into a jar and it's ready to use.

For each test, use 2 tablespoons of the liquid in a small glass. Try vinegar first, adding it drop by drop to the purple liquid. Watch the liquid change to rosy red. When it's red, add ¼ teaspoon of baking soda. The color changes again. Now it is green—the telltale color for a base.

Test different fruit juices. After checking with a grown-up, try cleaning supplies and different powders from around the house. You will find some that do not change the color of the liquid, for they are neither acids nor bases.

①

 ②

③

27

The colored chemical in cabbage juice has a special name. It is called an *indicator*. It indicates—that is, shows—acids and bases.

Indicators can also be made from flower petals. Some kinds change from red to green the way cabbage juice does. You might find some that change to other colors.

Collect petals from colored flowers such as blue iris, purple dahlia, violets, violet pansies, red tulips, daffodils. Soak each kind in a cup of hot water for an hour to get out the color. Then test each solution. Use a few drops of vinegar for the acid and a pinch of baking soda for the base.

Try the same test on juice from berries and from plums. You'll find many fruit juices that are indicators.

Acid Test Sticks

Indicator solutions are hard to keep. If you want indicators for your chem set, make test sticks from cotton swabs.

Put some red indicator solution from cabbage in a glass. Soak one end of some swab sticks in it until the cotton is red. Remove the sticks. Then make the indicator solution turn green by adding baking soda. Soak the other end of the sticks until the cotton is green. Dry the sticks and they are ready to use.

How Gases Behave

Imagine walking right through something that's moving, without feeling it or getting hurt. That seems to be a Superman stunt, yet you do it every day. Whenever you walk, you go through gases of the air.

The molecules in gases are very, very far apart, and they have no color. That's why you can't feel or see air. But you can see how the gases in it behave.

Invisible but Real

The gas molecules in air are always moving. Light a flashlight in a darkened room. Then watch the dust specks in the beam. They are never still. They keep jiggling because gas molecules keep hitting them while darting around.

Do the molecules ever change speed? Set a tray of ice cubes in the light beam and watch the dance of the dust specks. You see it slow down, so you know the gas molecules are slowing down.

Something else happens as air cools. The molecules draw closer together. Then the air contracts. Blow up a balloon and put it in the refrigerator. Look at it after an hour. Is the balloon smaller? If it is, you know the air inside has contracted. Hang the balloon in a sunny window and it will get big again as the gas molecules spread out.

What Smells Tell

Sometimes sniffing a smell will give you an idea of how fast gas molecules move.

Stand at one end of a hall with a friend at the other end. Have the friend open a bottle of perfume. You watch the time and note how long it takes for the smell to reach you.

It didn't take long, did it? The gas molecules moved pretty fast.

At the end of the experiment, be sure to close the bottle. If you don't, the perfume will dry up. It will *evaporate*. The liquid will turn into vapor or gas.

When any liquid evaporates, its molecules do not change. They just spread out in the form of gas.

From Gas to Liquid

"Shazam, shazam!" the magician says. And birds, coins, and flowers appear, right out of the air. It's a trick, of course. But you really can make something come out of the air. You can make one of its invisible gases turn into liquid.

There's always water vapor in the air, although you can't see it. When air is cooled, the vapor molecules draw together. They collect into drops of water big enough to see.

Fill a dry glass jar with ice. As the jar cools, drops of water collect on the outside. Dry off the jar and more drops show up.

The water on the jar comes from the air. It changes from gas to liquid as fast as you can say, "Shazam!"

Outdoors, the only gas in the air that turns to liquid is water. The weather is never cold enough to change any of the others. Indoors, scientists can cool air to a few hundred degrees below zero. They can make air so cold that all its gases turn to liquid.

Did you ever hear of LOX? It's rocket fuel. The L stands for liquid and the OX for oxygen. And that's what it is—liquid oxygen. After the gas is taken from the air, it is cooled to liquid and stored in tanks.

About one out of every five gas molecules in the air is oxygen. Most of the others are molecules of nitrogen. Nitrogen stays by itself most of the time, but oxygen is different. It combines with many other things. It's a very active gas.

An Experiment with Oxygen

When oxygen combines with iron, rust forms. You can use this fact to show how much oxygen is in the air.

Stuff some clean steel wool into a glass with straight sides. Turn the glass upside down and place it in a dish of water. Add a drop of food coloring to the water. Keep the experiment going for a week or so.

The steel rusts, taking oxygen from the air. That causes suction, and the water rises. It rises about 1 inch in a glass that's 5 inches tall. It fills a fifth of the glass, taking the place of the oxygen that was in the air.

A Heavy Gas

It was Grandpa's eightieth birthday. He said, "I'm going to put out the candles on my cake faster than you can say, 'Happy birthday.'"

And he did—with a small fire extinguisher that he took off the kitchen wall. No one could see anything come from it. Yet the candles went out—all of them!

Chemicals in the fire extinguisher had made carbon dioxide. This invisible gas puts out fires. It pours downward because it's heavier than air.

Carbon dioxide is easy to make. But you can't tell you have made the gas unless you test it with limewater. Clear limewater turns milky when carbon dioxide is added to it. You can probably get some at school.

To make limewater for yourself, use lime from a garden supply shop. Use the kind containing slaked lime. Stir a tablespoon of it into a small jar of water. Let it settle overnight. Then pour the clear liquid into another jar. Cover it and label it LIMEWATER.

Is It Carbon Dioxide?

Get two jars—a small one, and a tall one with a piece of cardboard for a cover. Into the small jar, put 2 tablespoons of limewater. Into the large jar, put 1 tablespoon of baking soda. Add ¼ cup of vinegar to the large jar and quickly put on the cover. As bubbles form and break, gas fills the jar. Now pour the gas into the limewater. It turns milky—proof that you have made carbon dioxide.

To test your breath, put 2 teaspoons of clear limewater in a glass. Blow into it through a straw and the limewater turns milky. That's because you breathe out carbon dioxide. Everyone does.

38

Bubbles Where You Want Them

Air or any gas will make a bubble. But there has to be something around the bubble to hold it together. The outside must be made of stuff that stretches, then keeps its shape.

What kind of substances do that? Finding them is a chemist's job. That's where the science of bubble making begins. And that's where the fun begins, too.

How Foams Form

Blow bubbles in plain water and they break. But the fizz in a soft drink turns into a foaming mass of bubbles. The soft drink has syrup in it, and that makes it sticky. As bubbles reach the top, the liquid stretches around them. It forms a skin that makes the foam last awhile.

A permanent foam can be made from rubber in a factory. While the rubber is a hot liquid, gas is bubbled into it. The rubber stretches around the bubbles. Then it cools and hardens, and the bubbles are trapped inside.

Plastic foams are made in the same way.

Bubble Gum Science

You know what forms a bubble gum bubble—your breath. But what is the gummy stuff made of? Take a piece of bubble gum from a pack. Press it flat and pull it to thin it out. The gum stretches like rubber—and no wonder. Usually there's some rubber in it.

In making bubble gum, rubber is heated and blended with wax, plastic, and flavoring. Vegetable oil is added to make the mixture soft enough to chew.

The gum makes a firm bubble skin, but do the bubbles last? Here's a chance to chew bubble gum for science and find out.

Blow a bubble gum bubble. Get it as big as you can without breaking it. Then set the bubble in a dish. As the air inside the bubble cools, the skin shrinks a little, but it doesn't break. See how long the bubble holds up. Does it last a week, or longer?

Test different kinds of bubble gum to see which makes the biggest bubbles. That kind has the most stretch and forms the thinnest film.

The Pop in Soda Pop

Before a bottle of soda is opened, you can't see any bubbles in it. Yet a gas is imprisoned in the soda. Since it is under pressure, the gas molecules are crowded together. Uncap the bottle and down goes the pressure. The gas expands and up come the bubbles.

What is in them? Capture some gas from a bottle of soda. Then test it with limewater to see if it's carbon dioxide.

First pour some limewater into a small jar. Take a flexible straw and fit modeling clay around it. Open a bottle of soda. Put the clay cap, straw and all, into the bottle. Then bend the straw so that the other end dips into the limewater. Gas from the bubbles will shoot into the limewater. What happens to the limewater?

Test bubbling soda with an acid test stick from your chemistry set. You'll find it's an acid. That's why it has a tangy taste. Test it again after all the fizz is gone. You'll find it's not an acid anymore. Now it tastes flat.

Suds That Stretch

Add soap or detergent to water and you have a great skin for bubbles. It's amazing how much stretch there is to soapy water. It can spread out into a film that is 5,000 times thinner than a human hair.

Some soapy solutions stretch more than others. A very sticky one makes a thin, strong film. That's the kind to use in making bubbles.

To make a sticky solution, mix 1 teaspoon of shampoo or dishwashing liquid with 2 tablespoons of water. To test the solution, dip a straw in it and blow a bubble. If the solution is too thick, add a little more water. If it's too thin, add a little pancake syrup.

You'll want to experiment with bubble makers, too. Try a straw with one end cut off at a slant. Also try a plastic cup with a hole punched in the bottom. Dip the top in the soap solution and blow through the hole in the bottom. A plastic bottle with the lower part cut off makes a good bubbler, too. So does a small funnel.

To make a bubble hoop, cut out the middle of a small Styrofoam plate. What's left is the hoop. Dip it in the bubble solution, then wave it through the air. To get six bubbles at once, dip a plastic six-pack can holder in the solution, then wave it.

Bubble Party

Why not ask your friends to join you for a bubble party? Tell them there will be bubbles to share and to spare.

You'll want all kinds of bubble makers for your friends and several pans for the soapy solution. Mix it in a pitcher, using four cups of water to eight tablespoons of liquid soap.

Before your friends try out the different bubblers, give them a few pointers. Tell them to blow gently and to keep the ends of the bubblers wet. If soap film touches anything dry, it breaks. When they try to catch and hold bubbles, their hands should be wet.

After your friends try out the different bubblers, have contests to see who can—

blow the biggest bubble

catch the most bubbles

hold a bubble the longest

use a funnel to blow a bubble with a flower inside

get the most bubbles from one film on a hoop

Win or lose, everyone will enjoy the contests.

For prizes, you can give jars of leftover bubble juice and bags of bubble makers.

Hurray for bubbles! And hurray for your chemistry set and the SCIENCE FUN you have with it!

3

7 03